Making Cards

IN A WEEKEND

Inspirational ideas and practical projects

JAIN SUCKLING

NEW
HOLLAND

Published in 2000 by
New Holland Publishers (UK) Ltd
London · Cape Town · Sydney · Auckland

Garfield House, 86-88 Edgware Road
London W2 2EA
United Kingdom
www.newhollandpublishers.com

80 McKenzie Street
Cape Town 8001
South Africa

Level 1, Unit 4, 14 Aquatic Drive
Frenchs Forest, NSW 2086
Australia

218 Lake Road
Northcote, Auckland
New Zealand

ISBN 1 85974 168 1

Designer: Peter Crump
Photographer: Shona Wood
Assistant Editor: Anke Ueberberg

Editorial Direction: Rosemary Wilkinson

4 6 8 10 9 7 5

Reproduction by PICA Colour Separation, Singapore
Printed and bound in Malaysia by Times Offset (M) Sdn. Bhd.

Making Cards

Cards

IN A WEEKEND

CONTENTS

INTRODUCTION

Everybody loves to go to the letterbox to see if the postman has been round and if any surprises are in store! There is nothing nicer than receiving a bunch of cards on a birthday or other special occasion, and in amongst those cards a specially designed, handmade one has great significance – someone has taken the time and trouble to create a small work of art.

Making and sending cards is a lovely way to keep in touch and show people you care. There is no excuse for not finding a reason! There is always a birthday, wedding, christening or engagement coming up, a new baby on the way; perhaps a friend is moving house or has just passed their driving test. You may want to send a "Sorry" card to someone to apologise for a misdemeanour or say "thank you" for a good turn. Invitations are special if they are handmade and can be adapted for all occasions that involve a party! And there are, of course, the annual cultural festivals and celebrations: Christmas, Easter, Mother's Day, Father's Day and Thanksgiving.

Valentine's Day is my favourite day of the year – it lends itself to all manner of cards with lots of hearts and love poems and all things sparkly and wonderful! You can also invent your own occasion. Perhaps someone has cooked you a lovely meal and you want to make a food related "thanks for dinner" card.

Handmade cards are far too pretty to put away. You can store them in a specially made memento box, stick them to your pin-board, frame them or simply leave them on the mantle-piece forever!

The idea of making a handmade card originates from Victorian times, before mass-produced, printed cards were available and when it was the only form of conveying your best wishes on someone's special event. Styles and techniques have changed over the years and this book attempts to show modern, sophisticated and contemporary projects using bright, strong colours, fun and unusual textures, and a variety of collage ideas alongside traditional methods.

I hope this book will be a useful tool to springboard some ideas. Remember, a card is a very individual thing – feel free to adapt the ideas in this book to add a distinctly personal touch for your friends and family.

Make cards that appeal to your sense of texture and design. Love and passion should inspire them! Making cards can be an addictive hobby – once you start you will not want to stop. After reading the projects, attempt the ones you will enjoy making. You may discover you already have lots of the bits and pieces required to make your chosen card at home, but make sure you have everything you need before you begin.

Cardmaking is very versatile as it uses so many different media: paper and card, fabric, paint, dried flowers and favourite photographs. The beach, the countryside, your garden, Aunt Flo's sewing box, haberdashery stores, car boot sales, charity shops, craft fairs – all these are great places to source and collect unusual bits and pieces. At last you can stop feeling guilty about being one of life's hoarders!

If you are unsure of a technique, refer to the "Getting started" section at the front of this book. Then let your imagination run riot and enjoy yourself!

Iain Suckling

GETTING STARTED

This chapter describes the tools and explains the general techniques used to make the cards in this book. Check that you have all the materials and tools you require before you begin so you don't get frustrated half way through! Once you have mastered a few of the projects, you will want to be creative and adapt things as you would like, happily using the materials and paper you have available, as well as the exciting paraphernalia that you will find everywhere once you start looking! Keep a special "card" box and as you discover things, store them in the box so when you want to begin making cards, you have all your treasures in one place.

BASIC EQUIPMENT

Paper shops and craft shops will stock most of the materials used in the projects. The basic tools and equipment to begin making cards are listed in detail below, but be sure to check the list of materials needed for specific cards before you start.

• **Paper and Cardboard:** When buying paper and card the abbreviations "mic" and "gsm" refer to various thicknesses and weights of the papers and cardboards. The abbreviation "mic" is used when describing thickness and is short for microns, i.e. 1000 microns equals 1 mm. The abbreviation "gsm" is used when describing the weight and is short for grams per square metre, i.e. a piece of 100 gsm paper measuring 1 m² weighs 100 grams. A good weight to use is 230-260 gsm as this will be easy to fold and will not be too flimsy.

• **Handmade papers:** ① Handmade papers are widely available in good stationery shops, artists' supply and crafts shops. There is a huge variety of colours and textures available, and you can also choose between paper with inclusions or without, and translucent or opaque paper. Of course you can also make your own handmade paper.

• **Funky papers:** ② Holographic card, metallic effect paper and card, textured and corrugated card and a range of other materials can be obtained from general and specialist stationery shops and artists' suppliers. Glitter-effect papers sometimes have a self-adhesive backing. Some high-street chains also offer pre-packaged selections of funky papers and card.

• **Paper sizes:** Standard sizes used in this book are A4 (210 x 297 mm/ 8¼ x 11¹¹⁄₁₆ in) and A5 (148 x 210 mm/ 5¹³⁄₁₆ x 8¼ in). A5, folded in half, gives you the standard size greetings card to fit a C6 envelope. Sheets of paper and card can be bought in larger sizes (A1 or A2) from specialist paper suppliers and cut to suit your requirements.

• **Cutting mat:** If you use cardboard, it retains score marks from a craft knife or scalpel, so you will need to change the blade frequently for accuracy. Using a cutting mat is much easier as it self-

❷

blade on a craft knife can cut into the surface of a plastic ruler and ruin your work. A paper guillotine is also useful, but not essential.

• **PVA adhesive:** This is a strong glue which forms a permanent bond when used on paper and board. It dries leaving a transparent finish.

• **Spray adhesive:** This is commonly used for sticking paper to paper or board as it has the great virtue of sticking firmly. Repositioning can be possible for up to 30 seconds after

❹

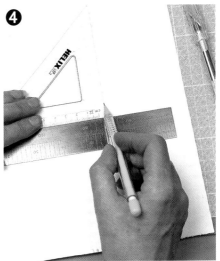

seals so your craft knife will not get stuck in previous score marks. The cutting mat allows the blade to sink into the material while cutting through the paper or card.

• **Craft knife:** A good, sharp craft knife is essential to keep your cut edges neat, so you may need to change your blade frequently. This also eliminates torn edges resulting from cutting paper with a blunt knife. Most craft knives come with blades which you can snap off when they become blunt. Scalpels can also be used – these are very sharp, so be very careful and have a supply of spare blades to hand if you are going to be doing a lot of cutting. It is very important to take great care when cutting – never cut towards your body. Have plasters handy just in case!

• **Scissors:** Do not use scissors reserved for cutting fabric on paper or card as the paper will blunt the blades. It is handy to have a couple of different sizes of scissors – a large pair for general work and a small pair, like nail scissors, for fiddly detail. Pattern-edge scissors can create amazing effects. Be careful when lining up the pattern from cut to cut ③. A pair of scissors with a smaller pattern can be used for details and a larger pattern for dramatic results.

• **Rulers:** A set square is essential, especially for cutting accurate right angles ④. A metal ruler is a good edge to cut against. If you haven't got one it will be worth investing in one, as the

❸

bonding two surfaces. Always protect the area surrounding the paper or object you are spraying with some new paper. Spraying into a box is a good way of protecting surfaces. Remember to use in a well ventilated room and carefully read the instructions on the can!

• **All-purpose clear adhesive:** This is a strong cement-like adhesive for sticking objects together. It is ideal for mixed media and fabric and dries leaving a transparent finish.

• **Glue sticks:** You can buy glue sticks with a fine tip which can be useful for writing. Glitter or embossing powder can be sprinkled over the glue.

• **Glitter glue:** This also comes in different thicknesses and many different colours. A fine tip applicator makes it easy to write out greetings ⑤.

• **Tape:** Cellophane tape, masking tape, doubled-sided tape, magic tape, sticky fixers and foam pads are all useful. Double-sided tape can be used instead of glue for more lightweight craft materials. Masking tape can be useful when spraying glue on specific areas of a card or blocking out certain colours when colouring. Sticky fixing foam pads can be used as an adhesive and also create a three-dimensional effect.

• **Cotton buds:** These are very handy for applying glue to small or fiddly items.

• **Tweezers:** Use tweezers to pick up small items such as quilled elements.

• **Sewing equipment:** Different size needles are useful for a variety of sewing effects. Threads can also be bought in different thicknesses. A thimble is handy for protecting your thumb or fingers when sewing through thick card.

• **Pencils:** Pencils must be kept sharp for accurate marking. An HB pencil is a good hard pencil for marking edges to be cut – use a softer pencil, such as a 2B, if you think you are going to make mistakes and need to rub the line out. A good eraser is also useful for this reason.

BASIC TECHNIQUES

CUTTING AND SCORING

You will need a craft knife, steel ruler and cutting mat to score or cut medium-weight cardboard or thick paper. Cut the card to the desired size using a set square and rule to insure the corners are square. On the outside of the cardboard measure the centre line where the card will fold and mark with a pencil. Make sure the pencil mark is parallel to the edge, or the card will not fold properly. Using the metal ruler and craft knife, lightly score over the pencil line but make sure only to score the top layer of the cardboard with your craft knife ①.

CUTTING A WINDOW

Use a ruler to measure the centre of the front of the card and mark lightly with a pencil. Then, using a set square, mark out where you wish to have the window, using the centre mark as a guide. Check the window is centred correctly by using a ruler to measure from the edge of the card to the edge of the window.

With the card opened flat on a cutting mat, carefully cut out the window using a ruler and sharp craft knife. Move the card around when cutting each edge so you are always cutting parallel to (never towards) your body. Cut with the window on the inside of the rule so you can see where the pencil lines begin and end. Take care not to extend the cuts beyond the corners of the window ②.

TORN EDGES

An attractive finish to your card or the design within your card is a torn edge, which is a characteristic of many handmade and water-colour papers. To achieve this effect, measure and mark with a pencil where you wish the torn edge to be. Fold the paper over along this line so that you have a crease to work with. Firmly hold down the ruler against the crease and tear the paper by pulling away or towards you. Do a little at a time and press the ruler down firmly to avoid ripping the paper where you don't want it to tear ③.

⑤

❶

❷

❸

MOUNTING A DESIGN

First you must make sure your design is cut square. Using a ruler and pencil, measure on the card where the design will go. Mark the corners so that you can register the glued design quickly and avoid messy edges. Position the top edge of the design on the card and press the design down towards you to avoid any creases or air bubbles. Leave to dry in a safe place.

RUNNING STITCH

Bring the needle and thread through to the right side, then insert the needle further along the material in a straight line parallel to the edge. Leave a smaller gap on the wrong side before bring the thread up on the right side again and repeat the process to create a running stitch ④.

❹

MAKING AN ENVELOPE

You can make special envelopes to fit your handmade cards in whatever media you wish, from beautiful coloured card to paper bags! Draw a plan before marking up your final piece. Use a pencil to mark the inside of the envelope. When measuring and marking the flaps, make dotted lines to indicate fold lines (or score lines if you are using card). You can also use the templates on pages 76 and 77, or disassemble an envelope of a suitable shape and size and use as a pattern.

Method:
Measure your handmade card and add 2.5 cm (1 in) to height and width. This

❺

❻

will be the base size of your envelope as it needs to be slightly bigger than the actual card for it to fit comfortably. Add a bottom flap which is three quarters of the basic height plus 2.5 cm (1 in). The top flap should be a quarter of the basic height plus 2.5 cm (1 in). Side flaps need to be 3 cm (1¼ in). All flaps should be tapered slightly. Mark the fold lines with a pencil and either fold or score using a rule and craft knife. Fold in the side flaps, apply glue to the edges of the bottom flap and fold it over on top of the side flaps. Fold down the top flap and use double-sided tape to seal the envelope before you send it ⑤.

PRESSING FLOWERS
At least two weeks in advance of making your card, press all the flowers, leaves and petals you wish to use in a heavy book between sheets of blotting paper or smooth tissue paper and leave to dry in a warm, dark and dry place. To avoid mould use less succulent flowers.

STAMPING AND EMBOSSING
Stamps can be bought in all shapes and sizes from shops or by mail order from specialist stamp manufacturers. Ink pads come in all the colours of the rainbow as well as in gold, silver and bronze. Special embossing ink pads can be used in conjunction with embossing powder to create a raised effect when the embossing powder is heated to melting point. When using stamps for decorating a card, make sure they are evenly covered with stamping ink ⑥.

AGEING
Use a heavy weight paper such as water colour paper. Wet the paper with a little water, then place two or three used tea bags on to the paper so the tea stains it. Coffee granules can also be used to stain. Use a wet paint brush to squash them into the areas you want to appear aged, or use a dry stencil brush to rub the granules into the paper.

COLLECTIBLES
Get collecting! Lace, shells, coins, old photographs and postcards, stamps, buttons, ribbons, raffia, feathers and much more can be found in flea markets, haberdashery shops or even your home. Keep things in labelled envelopes where necessary to make life easier. Similarly, make a file for magazine cuttings, wrapping paper and pieces of handmade paper ⑦.

GLITTER AND CONFETTI
Glitter stars, confetti in a variety of shapes from champagne glasses and numbers to Easter bunnies and angels,

bindis and holographic and glitter stickers are available from many stationery and card shops and are ideal for use in fabulous shaker cards or simply to sprinkle into the envelope for a special surprise ⑧!

GIFT TAGS
If you have leftover card, fabric, paper or other material from making a card, why not create a matching gift tag? You can also adapt elements of many of the projects in this book to a much smaller format and use them as gift tags.

DECORATING ENVELOPES
You can personalize envelopes in many ways: make one yourself from beautiful textured, handmade paper; wax-seal your envelopes; wrap the finished card and envelope in contrasting tissue or crepe paper and tie with gold cord; or embellish your envelope flap with small decorative elements from the card inside ⑨.

PACKING AND PADDING
At our studio we get hundreds of cards per week through the post and courier companies. Often the outside packaging gets damaged, so it is important to ensure all the goods we receive and send to shops are carefully padded to avoid damage. Nothing is more heartbreaking than to make a beautiful card and then to find it was broken on arrival at its destination. Gift-wrap your creation with tissue paper or cellophane to make it extra special, then send in a padded or stiff-backed envelope.

❼

❽

❾

HANDY HINTS BEFORE YOU BEGIN

Be kind to yourself – if all goes wrong, just try again!

~

The designs are only a basic guide – you can adapt most cards to suit a specific occasion.

~

Give yourself enough time to see a project through easily. Don't try to rush things – enjoy the process.

~

Be proud of your creations! If they turn out well you may want to suggest to the lucky recipient that they frame your card or stick it on the cover of an album.

~

If you regularly send cards to the same people you may want to make a special memento box for them.

~

Be adventurous – the beauty of handmade cards is that you can personalize them for the individual who is receiving them – whether they like cats, tulips, chocolate or whatever! You may like to use photographs and quirky sayings – something which will make the card unusual and unique.

~

Remember, children love to get in on the action! Encourage them to use their imagination – Father's Day, Mother's Day, Christmas, birthdays and thank you cards for Granny are all great opportunities for hands-on creativity!

~

Make sure there is no glue showing on your finished cards, as this makes them look cheap and messy.

~

If you have gone to lots of trouble to make a special card, you must remember to pack it properly if you send it through the post. Use a padded bag and bubble wrap. Perhaps wrap the card in nice tissue paper and tie a bow with some pretty braid: a gift in itself.

~

Finally, keep things simple. Don't clutter up your card with too many things and stick to a theme. Be adventurous with colour but, again, don't overdo it with too many combinations on one card. If in doubt – leave it out!

~

14

PROJECTS AND GALLERIES
FOR MAKING CARDS

EMBOSSED HEART

Pink, red and gold – the luscious colours of love! Embossing powder is available in many different colours and creates a stunning effect. Whispy handmade paper, red and holographic gold card and the lace effect of the embossed pattern make a splendid card to send to someone you really adore.

FUNKY ECLECTICA

1 Using the embossing stamp pad, stamp your design onto one half of the red card. Immediately sprinkle some gold embossing powder over the image before the ink dries, and shake off the excess powder back into its container. Heat the image from the underside over a toaster or use the embossing heat gun until the powder has melted. You will see this happen almost immediately. If the gold powder is not melting, your heat source is not hot enough.

YOU WILL NEED

Embossing stamp pad (tinted)
Rose stamp design
Red card, A4
Gold embossing powder
Embossing heat gun or toaster
Template (page 70)
Spray adhesive
Gold card, A5
Pink handmade paper, A4
Ruler
Pencil
Craft knife
Scissors with pattern edge
Greetings card blank, 250 gsm, 14 x 14 cm (5½ x 5½ in)
All-purpose glue
Plastic jewel

2 Using the template on page 70, cut out a heart shape from the embossed card. Apply spray adhesive to the back and stick onto the gold card. Now cut around the heart shape, leaving a 0.5 cm (¼ in) gold border.

3 Cut out a square of the handmade pink paper approximately 0.5 cm – 1 cm (¼ – ⅜ in) larger than the heart at its widest points. Apply spray adhesive to the back of the heart shape and stick centrally onto the pink paper square.

4 Cut out a square from the remaining red card, ensuring it is 1 cm (⅜ in) larger all around than the pink square. Use the scissors to achieve a patterned edge. Apply spray adhesive to the back of the pink paper square and stick centrally onto the red card.

5 Finally, cut out another piece of pink handmade paper slightly larger than your greetings card blank. Apply spray adhesive to the pink paper and stick onto the card blank, then trim along the edge to the size of the card blank.

6 Apply spray adhesive to the back of your collage and position on the card. Add the final touch to the embossed heart by glueing a plastic jewel to the top of the heart with all-purpose glue.

DECOUPAGE ANGEL

This art form from the Victorian era was used to decorate furniture, boxes and screens. A delicate composition and pretty colours make this lovely card reminiscent of past times, but you can also use images from magazines for a more contemporary effect.

ARTIST: AMANDA CAINES

1 Using the craft knife and ruler, cut a square measuring 10.5 x 10.5 cm (4¼ x 4¼ in) from the blue card blank.

— VARIATIONS —

Add a touch of glitter to the finished card. For an anniversary card use a cherub. A pastel background makes a more romantic card.

2 Cut out all the desired pieces of decoupage. You can use wrapping paper, tearsheets from magazines, or gardening catalogues. Cut some images with straight edges and corners to fit the sides and corners of the card. Arrange in groups by size or colour.

3 Choose a good central image for the card, depending on the occasion or the person the card is intended for. Using PVA or all-purpose glue, fix the angel – or whatever you have chosen as your main image – in the centre of the card.

4 Brush a small amount of PVA or all-purpose glue on the back of each cut piece and arrange everything around the angel, building up layers until you have a pleasing arrangement and well-balanced design. Trim any pieces which overlap the edges of the card. Allow to dry and present in a square white envelope.

5 You might like to try a lighter colour scheme on a portrait format, decorated with glitter glue, to achieve a different, more delicate look.

6 The decoupage images do not have to reach all the way to the edge of the card – try leaving a generous border of blank card around the arrangement to "frame" it.

STENCILLED CUPID

Stencilling is easier than drawing – stencil your chosen image and nobody will believe that such a professional and unique effect was created by you! The cupid is a great alternative to a heart for this sophisticated love card, and the antiquing effect makes it that much more special.

FUNKY ECLECTICA

1 Using a permanent ink pen, trace the outlines of the cupid template from page 70 onto a sheet of mylar. Trace the bow separately as this will be worked in a different colour.

Mylar (type of plastic used for stencils, available from stencil or art and craft shops)

Permanent ink pen

Template (page 70)

Picture glass (this should be larger than the cupid design itself)

Heat pen or craft knife

Stencil mount

Spare paper

Watercolour paper (minimum 300 gsm to avoid wrinkling)

Stencil paint in dark blue and purple

2 stencil brushes, medium size

Kitchen paper towel

White greetings card blank, 250 gsm, A5, folded in half

Pencil

Ruler

Sponge

A few coffee granules

2 tea bags

Hairdryer (optional)

Spray adhesive

2 Place the mylar onto the picture glass. When the heat pen is hot, trace over the design, then carefully push out the shape with your fingers. Alternatively, if your design is not too complicated, it can be cut out with a craft knife. You can also use a pre-cut stencil.

3 Spray the reverse of the stencil with a light, even coat of stencil mount, wait a few seconds allowing it to become tacky and blot onto a spare piece of paper to remove any excess glue. Place the stencil in position on your watercolour paper. Shake a small amount of blue stencil paint into the lid or pour into a dish. Dab the brush into the paint and work the paint into the bristles of the brush in a circular motion on a piece of kitchen paper to disperse the colour evenly. With the almost dry brush, colour the stencil. Slowly build up the colours, using a circular or a stippling motion. Remove the stencil carefully and reposition it to work the bow in purple, using a clean brush.

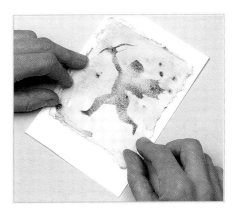

4 With a pencil, mark a rectangle close to the cupid on the water-colour paper, leaving approx. 0.5 cm (¼ in) from either side and approx. 1 cm (⅜ in) from top and bottom of the design. Position the ruler on the pencilled lines, put pressure onto the ruler with one hand and with the other pull the corner of the paper towards you to achieve a torn edge.

5 Lightly dampen the paper with a sponge, then gentle shake a small amount of coffee granules on top. Using a clean stencil brush, work the granules into the paper, leaving some granules undissolved. Place a couple of used tea bags on top and leave for half an hour to stain the paper, then remove the tea bags and dry with a hairdryer or leave to dry naturally.

6 When the paper is completely dry, lightly spray the reverse with spray adhesive. Wait for 10 – 15 seconds, then position on the greetings card blank. Place under a couple of heavy books until the adhesive is dry.

NINE ROSE PETAL HEARTS

The number nine signifies "forever" or "eternity" in Chinese culture and is considered auspicious for the celebration of birthdays and friendship, and red roses are a traditional western gift of love, making this a perfect Valentine's Day card.

ARTIST: CHIU MEI AU-YEUNG

1 Two weeks in advance, press the rose petals between blotting paper in the pages of a heavy book and leave to dry in a warm, dark and dry place.

YOU WILL NEED

9 pressed red rose petals
9 sheets mulberry paper in pink, lilac, purple, dark green, turquoise, earth green, yellow, orange, dark orange
Cocktail sticks
PVA glue
Textured white card, 250 gsm, A5, folded in half
Scissors

TIP

The torn paper squares should butt up against each other, but do not overlap them or the separate colours will not stand out so well.

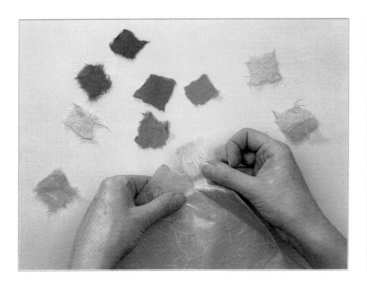

2 Measure and fold a 3 cm (1¼ in) square on one of the sheets of mulberry paper, then tear along the folds to make a rough-edged square. Repeat with each of the different colours.

3 Using a cocktail stick, apply glue to the back of one of the squares of mulberry paper and stick it to the top left-hand corner of the front of the folded white card about 1 cm (⅜ in) from each edge. Stick down the rest of the squares close to each other to form a 9 x 9 cm (3½ x 3½ in) multicolour square.

4 Using the scissors, cut each pressed rose petal into a heart shape to fit the 3 cm (1¼ in) squares of paper.

5 Apply glue to the back of the petal and stick to the middle of the top left coloured square. Repeat until all the squares are filled.

LOVE GALLERY

Gold swirly heart
A simple gold and red heart
on plain blue makes a
charming design.
Rowena Burton

Wire flower
Tracey's inimitable style is reflected here
in a wire flower on paper and gold net
with a pearl centre and raffled edge.
Tracey Anne Turner

Gold frame petal
A machine-stitched gold border is an
attractive setting for this petal cut into
a heart shape and placed on gorgeous,
textured white paper.
Nadia Moncrieff

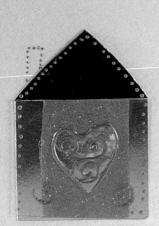

House of love
This happy house made from a simple, graphic
silver board cut-out is decorated with fabric pen
and glitter-effect fabric. *Lucy Thomas*

Perfect pansy
A pressed flower pansy, a patterned edge and good use
of simple colour combinations make this embossed
gold card a pleasure to behold! *Funky Eclectica*

Wooden daisy

The favourite daisy in yet another style. Wood, painted spring yellow, frames it beautifully with a ribbon detail. *RaRa*

Mother's day

Purple ribbon adds a rich finish to this antique-effect old favourite family photograph. An ideal birthday or Mother's day card. *Anke Ueberberg*

Sparkly heart

Sparkly fabric, craft paper, silver board and swirls of glitter pen make this unusual layered card ideal for a romantic gesture! *Lucy Thomas*

Daring damask

Shining effect damask paper and fabric pen were used to make this stylish and sensual romantic card. *Kathryn Ferrier*

Silver heart

A card for any occasion related to the heart! A kiln-fired clay heart, cleverly textured and painted silver. *Zoe Ryan at Biscuit*

BOUQUET OF TULIPS

Perfect for a birthday, for Mother's Day, as a "Thank You" card, or simply to say "Hello", this exquisite and colourful paper and wire collage card shows the time and care taken to make it and will convey your love and friendship to the happy recipient.

ARTIST: TRACEY ANNE TURNER

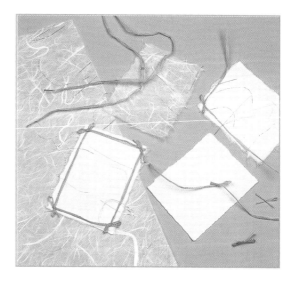

1 Tear a 9 x 7 cm (3½ x 2¾ in) rectangle out of the white cartridge paper and out of the white handmade paper, then glue together. Take two 25 cm (9¾ in) lengths of raffia and tie a bow near the centre of each, then glue the bows down on the inside edge of the handmade paper at opposite corners. Trim the excess lengths of raffia to fit the card and glue down. Make two separate bows from the left-over raffia and glue those down in the remaining corners. Put to one side.

YOU WILL NEED

White cartridge paper, A4
White handmade paper, A4
All-purpose glue
4 lengths of raffia, 25 cm (9¾ in) long
Scissors
Yellow handmade paper, A4
White organza, 10 x 10 cm (4 x 4 in)
Template (page 70)
Pencils in pink, blue, purple, orange, yellow and green
Craft knife or scissors
Gold plated jewellery wire, diameter 0.4 mm
Pliers
Blue ribbon, approx. 20 cm (8 in) long
Length of small pearls, 20 cm (8 in)
Small leaves from the garden
Yellow card, 250 gsm, A5, folded in half
Yellow envelope, C6

2 Draw two 8 x 5 cm (3⅛ x 2 in) rectangles onto the yellow handmade paper and cut out. Cut the corners off one of the rectangles to create a kite shape. From the second rectangle, cut a triangular shape to fit the lower part of the kite shape.

Apply a thin line of glue on the long edges of the triangle and glue in place on the kite shape. For extra decoration, cut an organza triangle slightly larger than the yellow handmade paper triangle. Place over the lower part of the kite shape, then fold and glue down the overlap on the back of the kite shape.

3 Draw 14 tulip heads and stalks onto the cartridge paper, using the template on page 70. Colour in six pink, two blue, two yellow, two purple and two orange tulip heads with the pencils. Colour the tulip stalks green and cut out the tulips. Make four or five golden swirls out of the jewellery wire using the pliers and tie a blue bow out of the ribbon. Cut one length of two pearls and one length of three pearls. Collect some tiny leaves from the garden or cut small leaf shapes out of a larger leaf.

4 Glue the kite shape onto the white rectangle made in step 1. Glue the flowers inside the pocket of the kite and add individual pearls, leaves and wire swirls. Glue the ribbon bow and the two lengths of pearls at the bottom of the bouquet and decorate with a single pink flower and two leaves, then glue the collage onto the front of the yellow greetings card blank.

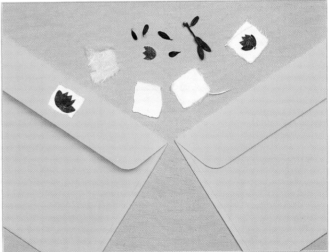

5 For extra decoration on the back of the card, tear a 4.5 cm x 3.5 cm (1¾ x 1⅜ in) rectangle out of the cartridge paper and white handmade paper, glue together, glue one pink tulip and two leaves to the centre and decorate the edge with raffia as before. Glue to the back of the card.

6 For the envelope, tear a 2 x 2 cm (¾ x ¾ in) square out of the cartridge paper and white handmade paper, glue together, decorate with a tulip head and two small leaves and glue onto the flap of the envelope.

NET AND WEDDING CONFETTI

Think of a wedding and your first thoughts might be confetti, rings and the bride's veil. This collage combines all these elements to make a beautiful card to keep, vividly reminiscent of the big day for the happy couple!

ARTIST: AMANDA CAINES

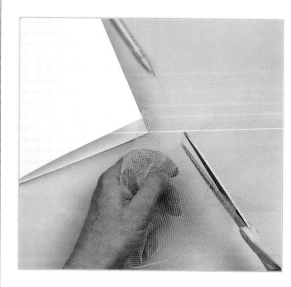

1 Fold and cut the white card to the desired size, using the ruler and craft knife. Cut the net fabric to approximately twice the size of the card to allow for gathering.

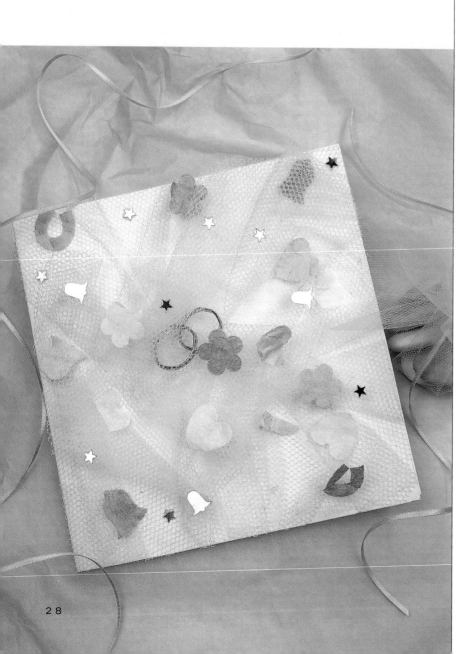

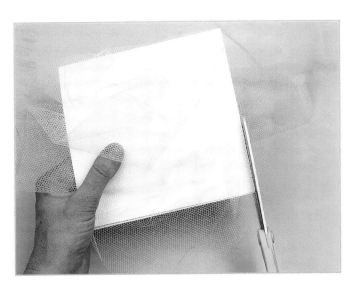

2 Spread clear glue all over the card. Gather the net fabric and gently press it in place on the card until the glue is dry. Trim off the excess net from around the edges, taking care not to cut into the card.

3 Interlock the wedding rings or place them side by side. Dot with glue using a spatula and place on top of the net in the middle of the card. Hold in place until the glue is dry.

4 Dot a little PVA glue on the back of the confetti pieces. Place them, glue side down, on the net, so that it looks as though they have been loosely scattered onto the net.

5 Glue stars and gold bells in place in the same way, spacing them evenly to give a balanced composition. Present in a silver, gold or brightly coloured envelope.

WEDDING GALLERY

Glorious stitching
Left: Gold Chinese leaf paper, orange tissue and a pressed primrose flower, edged with machine stitching, make a special spring wedding card.
Nadia Moncrieff

Embossed metal
An interesting alternative for the modern bride and groom: embossed aluminium metal can be left silver or sprayed with gold car paint as in our example.
Funky Eclectica

Cake congratulations
Subtle craft papers with petals and delicate stitching on the cake make a beautiful card. *Dawn Ireland*

Unique organza
Gold braid and divine embroidered material mounted onto board for a 3-D effect recreate the splendour of the special day. *Kate Twelvetrees*

Delicate decoupage

A pretty example of decoupage using bright colours and strong images for some old-fashioned romance.
Amanda Caines

Holographic heaven

The large card format lends itself to the strong silver holographic materials. A great example of simple yet effective design. *Kate Horeman*

Eastern flavour

The oblong format, bright pink card, mixed glitter colours, gold paper and a beaded Indian bindi make this an exotic and interesting wedding card.
Caroline Dent

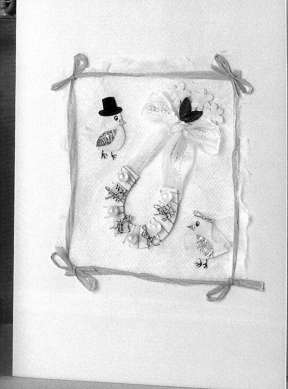

Wedding wonders

The cute image of love birds and a traditional "good luck" horseshoe embellished with pearls, raffia and ribbon combine to make a delightful congratulation!
Tracey Anne Turner

WEDDING CAKE

Whether you are a beginner or an expert with the needle, this is the card for you! A beautiful and elegant card, it is perfect for sending on the wedding day itself or for an anniversary. You could cut the cake from gold or silver paper instead. If you prefer to use your sewing machine, try the variation on page 30.

ARTIST: DAWN IRELAND

1 On the reverse of the handmade petal paper, measure and mark lightly with a pencil a rectangle measuring approximately 6 x 8 cm (2¼ x 3⅛ in), then tear along the marked lines. This will form the background for the wedding cake design.

YOU WILL NEED

Handmade petal paper, A4
Pencil
Steel ruler
Lilac plain paper, A4
Template (page 70)
Craft knife
Cutting mat
Glue stick
Small piece of gold paper
Needle
Metallic gold embroidery thread
White card, 230 gsm, A5, folded in half
Metallic gold envelope, C6

TIP

You can also achieve the sewing effect by drawing dotted lines with gold or silver pen.

VARIATIONS

Cut out a house shape or a pram in similar craft papers and you have another perfect greetings card.

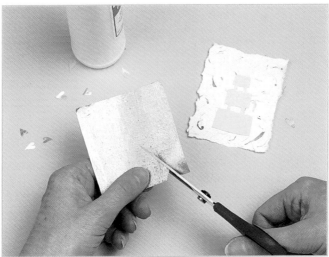

2 Using the template from page 70, draw out the wedding cake on a piece of the lilac paper. Carefully cut out the cake using the craft knife and cutting mat.

3 Glue the cake slightly lower than central onto the handmade petal paper. With the scissors, cut out a small heart from the gold paper. Glue in position on the petal paper at the top of the cake.

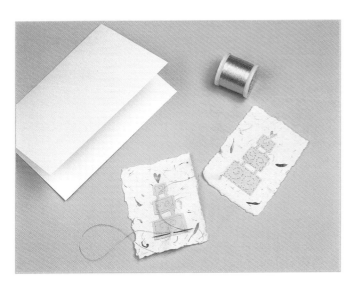

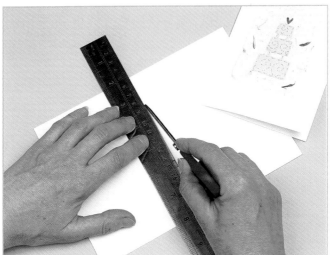

4 Faintly pencil the design from the template onto the cake shape, outlining each layer of the cake and adding swirls inside, then make evenly spaced holes with the needle before sewing. Using the needle, threaded with gold embroidery thread, work along the swirls and edges of the cake in running stitch.

5 Score and fold the card in half. Position the collage neatly on the front of the card and glue in place.

SILK PAINTED HOUSE

Silk painting is a traditional craft used on scarves and wall hangings. These miniature adaptations for the card format work perfectly for many different occasions. Flowers for birthdays, hearts for Valentine's Day, champagne glasses for celebrations – the list is endless. We've featured the house for a lovely, welcoming New Home card.

ARTIST: ROWENA BURTON

1 Stretch the plain white silk over the wooden frame, securing it on all sides with masking tape, so that it is smooth and taut.

YOU WILL NEED

A piece of white silk approx.
15 x 15 cm (6 x 6 in)

A frame (you can use a wooden picture frame), approx. 12 x 12 cm
(4¾ x 4¾ in)

Masking tape

20ml tube of Marabu Konturmittel
(gold contour liner) 084

Template (page 74)

Brush

Silk paints in Marabu karminrot (red)
032, Marabu mittelgelb (yellow) 021,
Marabu violett dunkel (purple) 051,
Marabu maigrun (green) 064, Marabu
mittelblau (blue) 052,

Wide double sided tape

Scissors

White, textured greetings card blank,
250 gsm, A5, folded in half

Envelope, C6

TIP

You could use drawing pins to secure the silk on the frame.
Alternatively, use an embroidery hoop to stretch the silk.

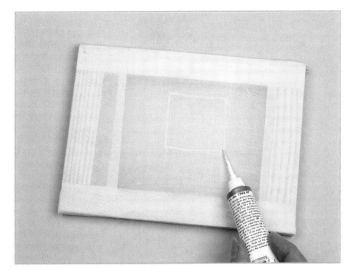

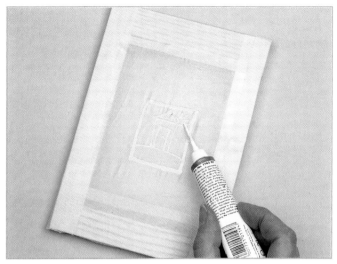

2 Using the tube of gold contour liner, draw a rectangle 4 x 4.5 cm (1½ x 1¾ in) in the middle of the silk.

3 Still using the gold contour liner, draw the house design in gold inside the gold rectangle. Alternatively, copy the template on page 74, place it underneath the silk when stretching it over the frame and trace the design.

4 Using the silk dyes, paint a red door, yellow front, purple roof, green hill and blue sky within the outlines. Leave to dry after applying each colour.

5 Apply double-sided tape to cover the back of the design. Carefully peel the silk off the frame and gently remove the masking tape. Cut out the design close to the gold outline. Peel the paper backing from the tape and stick the design in place on the front of the white card.

6 You can enlarge the design on a photocopier for a bigger card, or reduce it to make a smaller design suitable for a gift tag.

NEW HOME POP-UP

This card is easier to make than it appears. The perfect card for the momentous occasion of moving house, this 3-D card can be personalized or left stylishly simple for maximum effect.

ARTIST: ANKE UEBERBERG

1 Photocopy or trace the base and roof of the house from the templates on page 71 and cut out using the ruler and craft knife. Cut out the window openings. Place the house base template onto the dark green card and mark the fold lines, then draw around the whole template and pencil in the windows. Do the same with the roof template on the lime green card.

YOU WILL NEED

Template (page 71)
White paper, A4
Felt-tip pen
Ruler
Pencil
Craft knife
Dark green cartridge paper, A4
Lime green cartridge paper, A4
PVA glue
White card, 250 gsm, 12.5 x 12.5 cm (4⅞ x 4⅞ in)
Dark green ribbon, approx. 100 cm (39½ in) long

TIP

Create a decoupage or stencilled garden around the house, or simply use pencils to draw in trees and flowers. You can also stick translucent paper behind the windows for added interest.

2 First, gently score the fold lines using the ruler and knitting needle. Cut out the house base using the ruler and craft knife. Cut out the windows and the door opening and fold the door and the flaps along the scored lines. Do the same with the roof. Write your message onto the side of the roof parallel to the flap.

3 Glue the roof flap onto the inside of the house base as shown, with the message on the outside. Measure and lightly mark 6 cm (2¼ in) from either side of the fold of the white card, both in the middle and at the bottom, and glue down the flaps of the house base, lining it up with the bottom of the card.

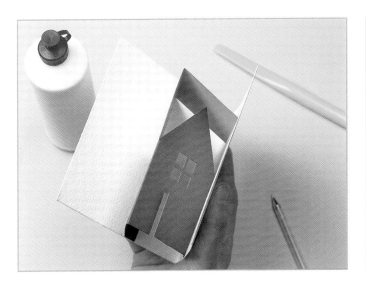

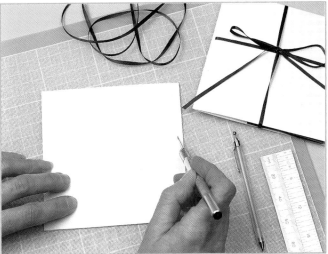

4 Check immediately that the house and roof fold down flat and straight. Make sure the roof does not stick out when the card is closed. Trim, if necessary, using ruler and craft knife. Leave to dry.

5 With the card closed, make a small cut close to the fold of the card and thread through the dark green ribbon (or whichever colour you prefer). Cross the ribbon at the back and tie a bow at the front.

ACETATE DAISY WINDOW

Simple graphics on clear material such as acetate create a subtle, contemporary look, suitable for any occasion. Pick your favourite image and simply photocopy it to make this stylish card, or choose an image appropriate for a specific occasion.

FUNKY ECLECTICA

1 Photocopy the daisy onto plain paper first to check the copy picks out as much detail as you would like. Photocopy the daisy onto the sheet of acetate.

YOU WILL NEED

Flat imitation flower (e.g. daisy or gerbera)
Acetate sheet, A4
Shiny silver card, A5
Steel ruler
Pencil
Craft knife
Cutting mat
Pale blue chromolux card, A5
All-purpose glue
Scissors
White, self-adhesive stickers

NB You will need to have access to a photocopying machine.

2 Using the steel ruler and pencil, mark out the frame shape on the reverse of the shiny silver card. Measure and mark a square of approximately 8 cm (3⅛ in) square on the outside. Measure 1 cm (⅜ in) in from each side and mark with the pencil. This will give you the thickness of the frame.

3 Cut out the frame using the craft knife and ruler. Take care not to cut into the corners. You can avoid this by cutting the corners first with the point of the craft knife.

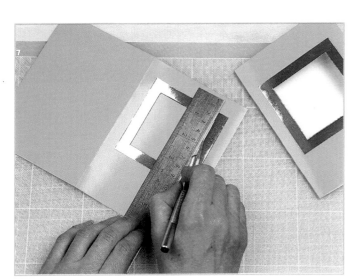

4 Score the blue chromolux card on the inside and fold in half to make the card. Glue the frame, silver side up, onto the front of the card just above the centre. Using the steel ruler and craft knife, cut out the chromolux card inside the frame to produce a window.

5 Cut out a square of at least 9 cm (3½ in) around the daisy print on the acetate sheet. Stick the acetate square to the the inside of the card using the white self-adhesive labels, making sure that the daisy is centered within the window.

GREETINGS GALLERY

Country cowslip
Clever use of pressed flowers on a gentle coloured paper are ideal to make this charming card. *Nadia Moncrieff*

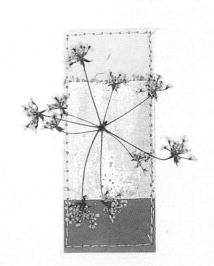

Holiday inspiration
All those favourite shells collected over time on special days can be made into a collage backed simply with sandpaper and netting for that beach effect!
Funky Eclectica

Fluffy cat
A wonderful idea and one of this artist's signature designs, the cat's fur tail flows over the mantelpiece – the bigger, longer and fluffier the better! *Kate Twelvetrees*

Knitted house
A new home with a quirk! Knitted and embroidered, this house is simple but effective on a plain background.
Mandy Jane

Ahoy!

Left: Rope, boats and painted balsa wood create a maritime moment for a special bon voyage card. *RaRa*

Little ladybird

This delightful, deep red card is gold-foil embossed and embellished with a fabric paint pen spot detail. *Kathryn Ferrier*

Celebrations

Champagne and ribbon on delicious hand-crafted paper with delicate inclusions is ideal for any celebration. *Funky Eclectica*

Wrapped baby

This sweet new baby card is made from fabric shaped into a blanket with a toy and dummy found in a junk shop! *Bizara*

STORK MOBILE

The movement created by dangling the stork and its baby bundle from a gold thread is simple but very effective. The cut-out shape could be simplified to a rectangle if preferred.

ARTIST: TRACEY ANNE TURNER

1 Using the template on page 72, draw a cloud shape onto the front of the card blank and cut out with a craft knife.

YOU WILL NEED

Pale blue greetings card blank, 250 gsm, A5, folded in half

Templates (page 72)

Pencil

Craft knife

Cutting mat

White card, 9 x 9 cm (3½ x 3½ in)

Orange pencil

Gold crepe paper, 9 x 9 cm (3½ x 3½ in)

All-purpose glue

Pale blue handmade paper, 9 x 9 cm (3½ x 3½ in)

Scissors

Needle

Gold thread, approx. 30 cm (12 in)

Gold-plated jewellery wire, diameter 0.4 mm, approx. 15 cm (6 in) long

Pliers

Pale blue envelope, C6

TIP

We have used blue card but you many want to use pink for a baby girl. The stork could be cut from metallic card, so that it will catch the light as it swings about.

2 Using the templates from page 72, draw the stork and its wing onto the square of white card. Draw on the eye. Colour the stork legs orange, then cut out the stork and the wing using the craft knife.

3 Using the craft knife, cut out a beak shape from the gold crepe paper and glue in place on the cut-out stork. Cut out a wing tip shape from the gold crepe paper. Glue onto the wing, then glue the wing into place on the stork's body.

4 Fold the square of blue handmade paper in half. From the folded edge draw a bag shape using the template on page 72 and cut out with scissors. Make a tiny hole at the top of the bag with the needle, then thread a 15 cm (6 in) length of gold thread through and tie in a bow.

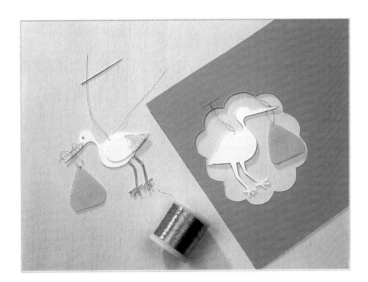

5 Glue the "handle" of the bag to the back of the stork's beak. Make a tiny hole in the stork's back. Thread a 15 cm (6 in) length of gold thread through it and tie in a knot. Dangle the stork by glueing the knotted end of the thread to the inside top of the card and secure it by glueing a tiny strip of card on top.

6 Draw three simple flower shapes onto the leftover handmade paper, using the template on page 72, and cut out with the craft knife. Glue to the bag, back of the card and the envelope flap. Cut three tiny circles from white scrap paper and glue to the middle of the flowers. Finish with a gold wire bow, twisted into shape with pliers and glued above the cloud shape.

AQUARIUM SHAKER

Will the cat catch the fish or only get the bones? Shake this exciting card designed for cat (or fish) lovers and see the holographic fish sparkle in the light. A great card for children, too, it can be adapted for special occasions using anything from stars to Easter bunnies.

FUNKY ECLECTICA

1 Ink the frame stamp and stamp firmly onto a sheet of white paper. Leave to dry, then apply spray adhesive and stick onto a piece of polyboard. Using the steel ruler and the craft knife, trim the polyboard close to the outside of the stamped design and cut out the centre to produce a window.

2 If you are using small fish stickers, peel them off the backing sheet and stick them onto coloured card. Cut them out with the scissors. You could also use nail scissors for this.

3 Position the frame on the greetings card blank along the fold line and mark the outline and the inside window with a pencil. Trim the card to size and cut out the window from the front of the card using ruler and craft knife. Put to one side.

4 Apply spray adhesive to the front of the frame and firmly press onto one piece of acetate. Trim off the excess around the edge of the frame. Place the frame face down onto a surface and position the fish, picture side down, inside the frame. Using the template on page 75, cut out some seaweed shapes from the coloured tracing paper, spray one side with glue and stick them onto the second piece of acetate.

5 Apply all-purpose glue to the back of the frame and position onto the seaweed-decorated acetate, creating a clear pocket with the fish inside. Trim off any excess around the frame. Glue the frame in position exactly over the window of the greetings card blank. Stamp the cat inside the card, so that it appears to look through the fish tank.

CARDS AS GIFTS GALLERY

Crazy daisies
These flower hairgrips, handmade from
painted buttons and stuck into lime-
coloured funky foam, are a fantastic,
original idea by this artist. *Emma Angel*

Sweet cone
Bright colourful papers
and sweeties – who would
not enjoy such a gift!
Funky Eclectica

Bunny girl
Part of a commercially available set,
this is an innovative idea, threading a
handmade bracelet through rivets
in the card. *Emma Angel*

Golden bookmark
An elongated shape cut out with pattern edge scissors,
this metal bookmark is embossed on gold paper and
finished with a bow. *Funky Eclectica*

Spangly tree

A Christmas card doubling as a
decoration, easily made with shiny
stars, silver snowflake stickers and
layers of stiff, coloured mirror
paper. Complete with a
ribbon at the top.
Funky Eclectica

Heart necklace

A seductive idea: the heart necklace echoes
the heart background and adorns a glamorous
woman's neck. A perfect gift card! *Emma Angel*

A cute purse – for cute things

An iconic image, sweet buttons and mirrors form a
lovely girly card with this Chinese fabric purse.
Emma Angel

Groovy key ring

This sewn key ring can have your favourite
actress, popstar of friends inside.
Emma Angel

FINGER PUPPET CLOWN

Is it a card or is it a toy? A fun idea to send to the little ones in the family, this card can be made using whatever colours and materials you can conjure up from your box of collected bits and pieces.

FUNKY ECLECTICA

1 Using the template on page 73, draw the shape of the clown onto the white card. Use a biro or felt-tip pen to get a good strong outline.

TIP

Instead of a circle of bright funky foam, you may wish to add a pom-pom or a bell to the top of the clown's hat. You could use glitter pen to decorate his hat and belt. Finally, red fingernails make fabulous clown shoes!

2 Cut out the template and draw around it onto the back of the flesh-coloured card. Cut out the shape.

3 On the template, mark out the hat, the clown's top and shorts with the fingerholes, the ruffle, belt, cuffs and hatband. Cut these into sections and use them as templates for the clown's clothes.

4 Using the templates, draw around each one on the desired coloured sheet of funky foam and cut out the sections. We have used purple for hat and top, white for hatband, mouth, ruffle, cuffs and belt and red for the trousers, but you can use any other colour combination you have available. Make sure you have each template the right way up.

5 Now, using the flesh-coloured clown shape as a base, start glueing the pieces of funky foam in the relevant places. Once all sections are glued in place, you can draw around each section with the black permanent pen to give the clown a more cartoon-like character.

6 Cut out the holes for the fingers into the shorts. If you want to add fun fur, make the holes slightly bigger than your fingers. Spread a line of glue around each of the holes, stick down the strips of fun fur and trim as necessary.

7 Cut out four small circles from the red funky foam and a mouth shape from the white. Glue these in position, using two of the red circles for buttons, one for the hat and one for the nose. Draw around the edges of the buttons with black permanent ink pen. Colour the ears orange with the felt-tip pen. Write your message on the back.

EMBOSSED METAL HEARTS

Embossed metal gives an artistic and charming effect. This romantic cherub and heart card lends itself to this medium, but you can use any other suitable line drawing to adapt the card to your own requirements. Have a go – it's easier than it looks!

Funky Eclectica

1 Place the folded greetings card blank on the aluminium sheet and draw around it with the point of a wooden skewer to make a rectangle of 15 cm (6 in) long and 10.5 cm (4¼ in) high. Press firmly to score a clear line into the foil.

TIPS

You can include a message on the card, but remember that the scoring is done from the reverse of the card, so any words will have to be written in mirror writing.

Spray the foil with gold paint for a Golden Wedding Anniversary card (see gallery pages 30-31).

2 Using the scissors, trim off the excess foil just outside the scored outline. Take care not to cut yourself on the sharp edges of the foil.

3 Inside the first rectangle, score another one measuring 10 x 6.5 cm (4 x 2½ in) on the same (reverse) side of the foil, to create an equal border all around the card. Score a zigzag pattern within the border and add small circles inside each triangle.

4 Trace the design from page 74. Lay the tracing paper over the reverse of the foil and, using the border to position the template, score the design onto the aluminium sheet in a fluid movement. Add hearts and small circles as desired.

5 Now turn the foil over, and, still using the skewer, draw along either side of any key lines of the picture again to highlight them. Score a series of short vertical lines all along the very edge of the foil to create a border decoration. Glue the foil to the front of the card blank.

CONCERTINA STARS

Sparkly, glittery silver – we love this idea! This unusual card is not as complex as it appears, and the matt silver and gun metal card combined with the glitter glue finish all add to the seasonal effect. It also has lots of space for greetings and messages.

FUNKY ECLECTICA

YOU WILL NEED

3 matt silver card squares, 13 x 13 cm (5⅛ x 5⅛ in)
Long piece of cream card, 280 gsm, 70 x 13 cm (28 x 5⅛ in)
Pencil
Steel ruler
Craft knife
Template (page 75)
White card
Paper glue stick/all-purpose glue
Shiny gun metal/dark silver card, A4
Scissors
Silver glitter glue pen

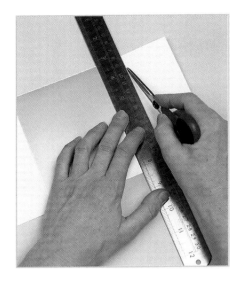

1 Using one of the matt silver squares as a guide, mark 13 cm (5⅛ in) squares along the cream card strip. Score along these lines gently using the steel ruler and the back of a craft knife or scissor blade. Fold along the scored lines to create a concertina effect. You will be left with a small fold at the righthand end.

2 Using the template on page 75, cut out a star shape from the spare card. Rule a line down the centre of the star shape. Align the pencil line with the fold line of the short fold, centered between top and bottom, and draw around the star shape with a pencil.

3 Cut out the righthand half of the star on the short fold and open out, then glue down the short fold on the front. Glue the first of the matt silver squares on top. This will be the front of the card. Next, glue down the remaining two matt silver squares on alternate squares along the concertina.

4 Using the star template, cut out three stars from the shiny gun metal card. Outline the stars with the silver glitter glue pen and add extra decoration. Leave to dry overnight.

5 Glue the first star in position exactly on top of the fold-out star shape on the top leaf. Then position the remaining two stars exactly behind the first on the other two folds, mark lightly with a pencil where they will go, apply glue and stick them down. Finally decorate the front of the card with extra glitter swirls. Send in a stiff-backed or padded envelope.

SEAHORSE STAMPS

Stamps can be purchased through all good craft stores and by mail order. They are easy and fun to use, and you can make the design as basic or as complicated as you choose. This is an ideal card to make with children. Simple repeating patterns on bright backgrounds often work best.

FUNKY ECLECTICA

1 Using the stamp and ink pad, stamp seahorses on a piece of orange card, leaving a gap between them. Put to one side to dry.

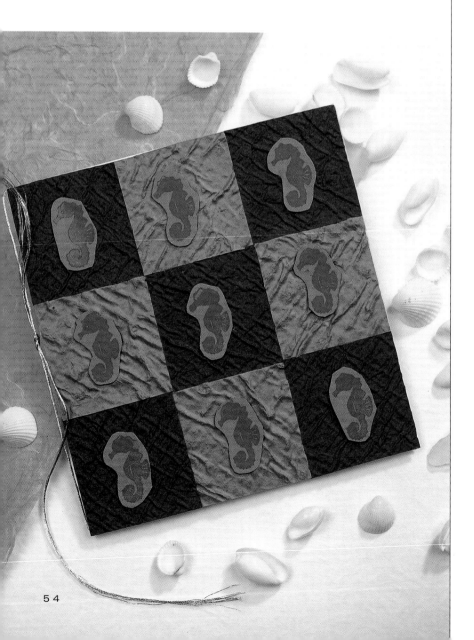

TIP

Try using different kinds of handmade paper, such as petal or rice paper in varying colours, for unusual effects.

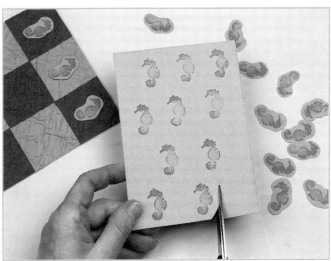

2 Cut nine 4½ cm (1¾ in) squares from the handmade paper – five of one colour and four of the other. Glue them onto the greetings card blank, starting in one corner with the colour of which there are more squares, continuing using alternating colours to achieve a chequerboard effect. Textured card is easier to use than flat card as it covers up any gaps between the squares.

3 The stamped seahorses should now be dry. Cut each one out with the scissors, following the shape of the seahorse and leaving a small orange border. Glue the seahorse shapes onto the card, one in each square.

4 Insert the turquoise tracing paper into the card and tie a coloured cord around the spine to hold it in place. Trim off the ends of the cord at the bottom of the card or tie it in a bow to sit centrally on the spine.

5 This technique can be adapted to suit special occasions or themes, using many combinations of coloured card and stamp designs. The stamp should be small enough to fit the paper squares. Contrasting colours make an eye-catching design.

BIRTHDAY GALLERY

Funky fishes
Holographic fish stickers and squares of funky foam create a seaside flavour. *Funky Eclectica*

A taste of the country
This collage of hand-picked, pressed flowers and a wonderful combination of purple papers will be a joy to receive. *Chiu Mei Au-Yeung*

Space odyssey
Silk painting at its best! This great rocket image is a perfect birthday surprise for all ages. *Rowena Burton*

Fimo fun
Various textured, layered papers, torn edges and a varnished fimo square make a bright background for a fimo detail. *Jana Pana*

Unusual stamp collection
This male-oriented card with bird feathers, foreign stamps and toy garden tools is ideal for Father's Day as well as Grandad's birthday! *Funky Eclectica*

Birthday parcel

This 3-D dangly parcel was made in the same way as the stork mobile on page 42. *Tracey Anne Turner*

Sweet honesty

Honesty and black-and-white graphic details say "good luck" feng shui-style to those fashion-conscious friends! *Lucinda Beatty*

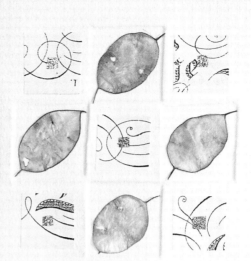

Pandamonium

Press me and I squeak! The cuddly felt panda on this fun card is hand-sewn, and the number is embossed on metal. *Funky Eclectica*

No 4

Balloon stickers and carefully dotted ink from an acrylic pen in subtle combinations of colours make a stunning child age card. *Julie By Design*

Dreamy daisies

Three daisies in a row on coloured tissue paper are ideal for a cute card or a special gift tag. *Funky Eclectica*

QUILLED FLOWER

This intricate quilled flower card makes a lovely "thank you". The traditional craft of paper lace can be used to create stunning, delicate patterns and motifs. This project is perfect for nimble fingers.

ARTIST: ANKE UEBERBERG

1 Score and fold the yellow card. Cut out a square 2 cm (¾ in) in from the edges all round to make a frame. Score and fold the blue card and trim 3 mm (⅛ in) off all open sides. Apply a thin line of glue along the fold line of the blue card and stick down just to the right of the fold line inside the yellow card.

YOU WILL NEED

Yellow card, 250 gsm, 9 x 18 cm (3½ x 7 in)
Steel ruler
Craft knife
Pencil
Eraser
Blue card, 250 gsm, 9 x 18 cm (3½ x 7 in)
PVA glue
Quilling tool or round pencil
White, orange and yellow quilling paper
Toothpick
Tweezers

TIP

If you want to send the card in the post, use a padded envelope or cushion the flower design with a piece of bubble wrap. If you present the card in person, you might want to embellish the envelope with a tiny quilled flower on the flap.

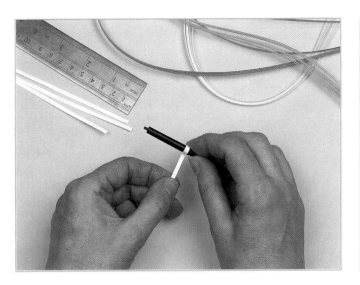

2 To make the petals, tightly wind a 15 cm (6 in) strip of white quilling paper around the middle of the quilling tool. Ease off and leave to unwind to the desired size.

3 Pinch one end of the loose coil to make a teardrop-shaped petal. Fix down the loose end of the strip with a dab of glue – use a toothpick or matchstick for this. Make another five petals in this way.

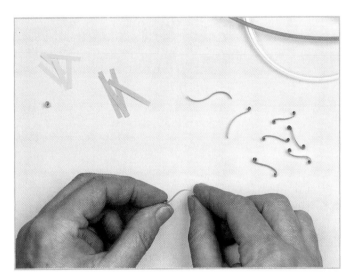

4 Make the orange curls by bending the ends of a 3 cm (1 in) strip of quilling paper in opposite directions using you fingernail, then roll tiny curls between thumb and forefinger. Finally, make the centre of the flower out of a 1 cm (⅜ in) strip of yellow quilling paper, rolled tightly between thumb and forefinger. Stick down the loose end with a dab of glue.

5 Starting with the centre coil, pick up each quilled element with the tweezers, dab spots of glue on the underside using the toothpick and position on the blue background within the yellow frame. Next, position the orange curls at even intervals, radiating out from the centre. Finally, stick down the white petals.

FELT CHRISTMAS TREE

*Christmas time is not complete
without a tree! This three-dimensional
felt cut-out appeals to children and
adults alike, and you can personalize
the tree with the materials you have
to hand. Instead of bells, you could
use gold buttons or gold-coloured
confetti, hole-punched from gold
foil or paper.*

FUNKY ECLECTICA

YOU WILL NEED

White card for template
Template (page 75)
Craft knife
Dark green felt, 18 x 9 cm (7 x 3½ in)
Biro
Scissors
Needle and light coloured thread
Wadding or foam
Pencil
Small piece brown felt, 2 x 1.5 cm (¾ x ½ in)
Gold bells
All-purpose glue
Small piece red shiny card
Green greetings card blank, 280 gsm, A5, folded in half
Gold star

1 Using the template on page 75, draw a Christmas tree on a piece of white card. Cut out using a craft knife.

2 Fold the green felt in half to make two layers, place the template on top and draw around it with the biro. Cut out the double-layer tree shape using the scissors.

3 Sew the two halves of the tree together with a simple running stitch along the edges. Stop sewing at the base of the tree, leaving a large gap.

4 Fill the tree with wadding or foam, using a pencil to push the stuffing right into the corners. Next, tuck the small rectangle of brown felt in at the base to make the tree trunk. Finish sewing round the tree shape to enclose the wadding and secure the tree trunk.

5 Glue the bells onto the tree. Cut a pot shape from shiny red card. Glue the star at the top of the card, sticking out over the top as shown, and glue the pot down at the bottom. Position the tree between pot and star and glue down.

SEASONAL GALLERY

Shiny foils

Save all those sweet foil wrappers to create
a bright, shiny collage egg, seen through an
oval window with a tidy border.
Funky Eclectica

Happy Easter

A hand painted egg
and felt borders
mounted on material
make this a lovely
representation
of Easter.
Alison Orr

Easter chicks

Fluffy feathers and chirping chicks are
perfect for Easter. *Amanda Caine*

Cool elegance

Cream-coloured, clean and fresh, this embossed watercolour
paper is beautifully decorated with delicate gold lines and a
simple, corrugated beige paper detail. *Lucinda Beatty*

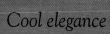

Crowning glory

s 3-D crown made from high quality craft paper and dangled on ld thread with wire details on top and bottom makes this card a special addition to the mantelpiece. *Tracey Anne Turner*

Pudding fun

Alternating orange and green, textured, handmade paper squares and an unusual pudding stamp made by the artist create this simple yet effective design. *Funky Eclectica*

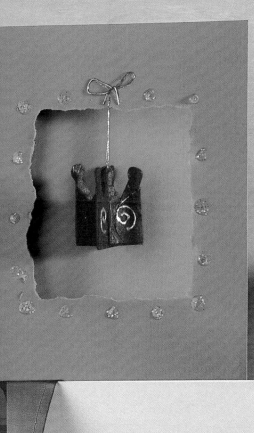

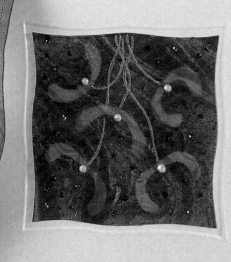

Sweet mistletoe

Lovely mistletoe adds a romantic flavour to this seasonal greeting. A clean-cut use of fabric pen works wonders! *Kathryn Ferrier*

Shimmering Christmas

Use crazy holographics for a crazy Christmas card with great colour combinations for a startling effect. *Funky Eclectica*

CHRISTMAS CRACKER TOKEN HOLDER

Christmas conjures up images of bright and sparkly textures. This cracker card, made with shiny red foil and gold glitter, is both fun and festive. Simply put your greeting inside or use it to present a cheque or gift voucher.

FUNKY ECLECTICA

1 Cut a piece of red shiny card to measure 26 x 25 cm (10¼ x 9¾ in). Using the scissors and steel ruler, gently score the card at 10.5 cm (4⅛ in) and 21 cm (8¼ in) from the lefthand long edge. Take care not to actually cut the card.

2 Fold the card along the scored lines, apply glue to the small overlap and stick down the large overlap on top. Leave to dry, then using the craft knife, cut a V-shape about one fifth of the way from the end of the tube. Do the same at the other end of the tube. Turn the tube over and repeat to make the cracker shape.

3 Cut a zigzag line down the middle of the cracker so it is now in two parts. Cut a strip of white card measuring 3 x 25 cm (1½ x 10 in) and score at 10.3 cm (4¹⁄₁₆ in) and 20.6 cm (8¼ in). Glue as before to make a smaller sleeve.

4 Glue the white sleeve in place inside one half of the cracker, halfway in. This will ensure the two halves of the cracker will stay in place.

5 Decorate the edges with the glitter glue pen for gold piping and glue on the stars and jewels. The glitter pen should disguise any marks made by the scissors or the craft knife. Leave to dry overnight. All that remains is to pop the token or voucher inside.

DRIVING TEST COLLAGE

Little toy cars are ideal for congratulations cards like this one. Of course it could also be a birthday card for the car enthusiast amongst your friends. Get into the habit of picking up small 3-D toys from jumble sales and junk shops – they might come in handy one day.

FUNKY ECLECTICA

1 Cut out a rectangle of red glittery paper 8 x 4 cm (3 x 1½ in). It should be just a little bigger than the toy car. Peel off the backing and stick at the top of the card at an angle.

Glittery red paper (self adhesive)

Scissors

Ruler

Black greetings card blank, 250 gsm, A5, folded in half

White piece of card or thick writing paper

All-purpose glue

Small piece silver card

Hole punch

Miniature keys

Piece of string

Small toy car

Round, red, yellow and green stickers

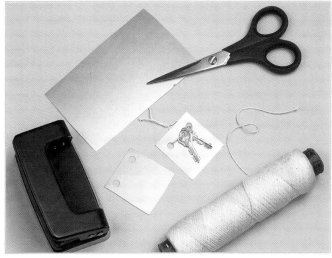

2 Cut out six small strips of white card about 3 cm long and 0.5 cm wide (1½ x ¼ in) and glue them in a curve just below the red glittery rectangle. Leave equal gaps between the strips to create a "pedestrian crossing", and leave a bigger gap in the middle.

3 Cut out a rectangle of silver card just bigger than the miniature keys. Using the hole-punch, make two holes at the top. Thread the string through the keys, then through the card, and tie a knot at the top of the string, leaving enough slack for the keys to dangle.

4 Glue the knot of the string onto the middle of the red glittery paper. Glue the silver card in place overlapping the bottom of the red paper at a slight angle.

5 Glue the car in place on top of the knot. Add the traffic lights.

6 Instead of a toy car, you could use a car-shaped eraser and spray it silver or any other appropriate colour.

OCCASIONS GALLERY

Shining angel
A decoupage cherub makes an angelic centre for this clever tag-type card. Glitter on metal creates a spangly effect, finished with a colourful orange bow. *Amanda Caines*

Lily-white
Silver corrugated card is used as a background for a lily fashioned from craft foam. Ideal for a birthday or a sympathy card. *Jan and Di*

Spiritual patterns
Top: A gorgeous ethnic effect is created here with ingenious use of glitter and a sewing machine in a spiritual combination of colour swirls: a little piece of art! *Amanda Hallam*

Paper parcels
This handmade collage of tiny parcels tied with cotton on pretty paper, cleverly juxtaposed with a lovely typographic surround, requires a lot of patience! *Susan Coomer*

Ethnic mix
Etched metal, glitter, sari material and
braid combine beautifully to make a special
card with an ethnic vibe. *Taro Taranton*

Precious jewel
Shiny silver mirror board, fabric pen swirls
and dots, glitter glue and a clear glass bead on shimmery
material form a strikingly modern collage. *Lucy Thomas*

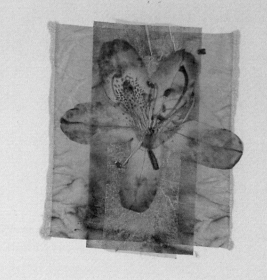

Daisy fun
Fun fur in bright orange combined with a paper daisy
is a perennial favourite and very simple to make.
Funky Eclectica

Petals and paper
Hand-painted tissue paper, gold paint and a beautiful
pressed flower from the English country side create a
delicate, natural effect. *Claire Lucas*

TEMPLATES

The templates shown here are actual size. All can easily be reduced or enlarged on a photocopier, but remember to adapt the size of the card to the size of the item you plan to use on it. Dotted lines indicate fold lines.

Embossed heart
(see page 16)

Stencilled cupid
(see page 20)

Bouquet of tulips
(see page 26)

Wedding cake
(see page 32)

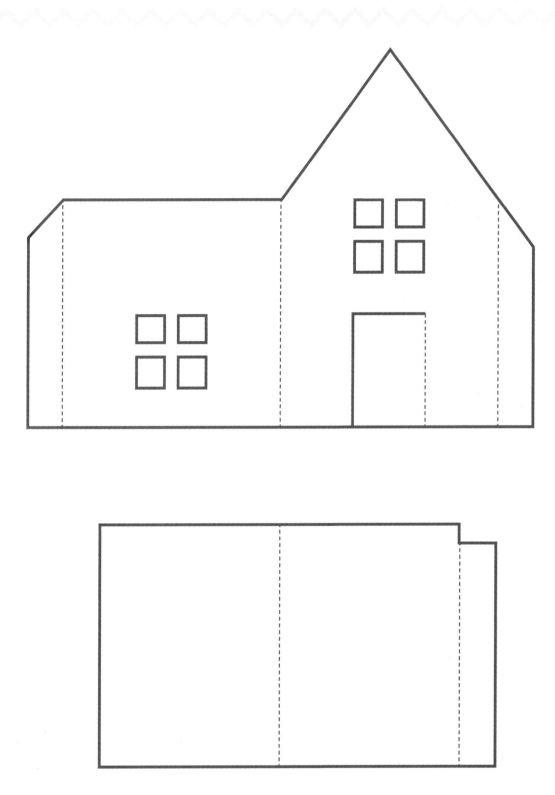

New home pop-up
(see page 36)

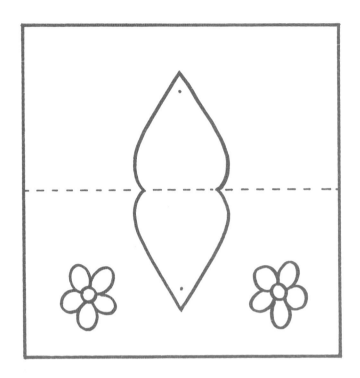

Stork mobile

Stork's bundle, flowers, cloud cut-out,
stork and wing (see page 42)

Finger puppet clown
(see page 48)

Embossed metal heart
(see page 50)

Silk painted house
(see page 34)

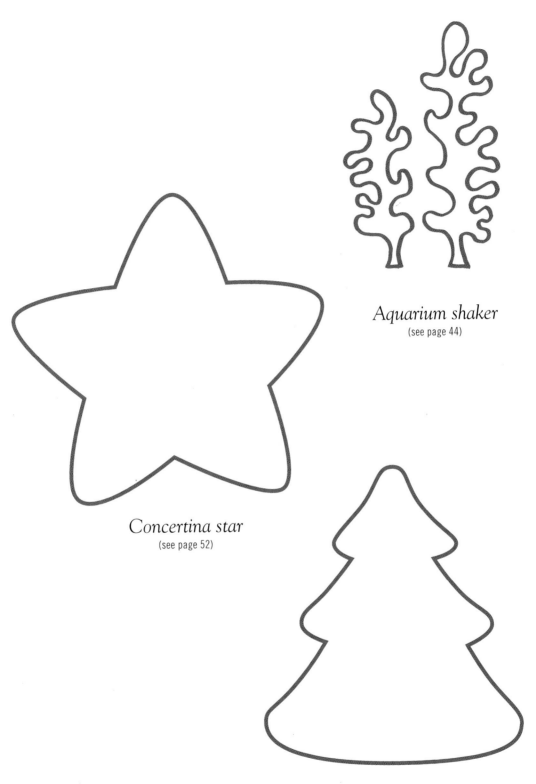

Aquarium shaker
(see page 44)

Concertina star
(see page 52)

Felt Christmas tree
(see page 60)

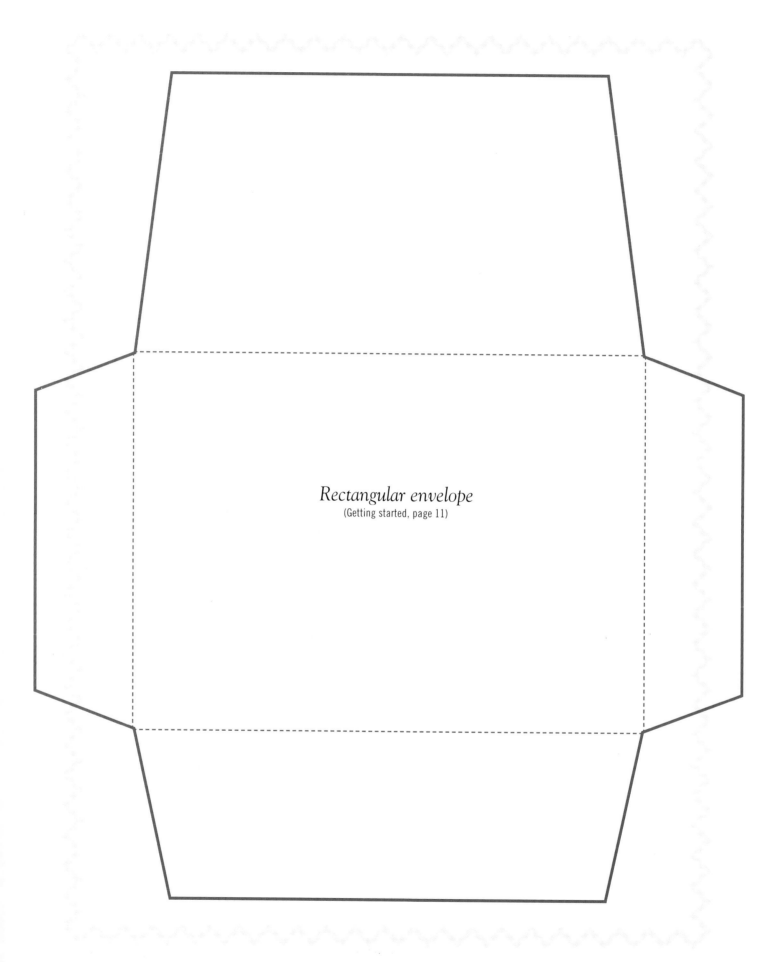

Rectangular envelope
(Getting started, page 11)

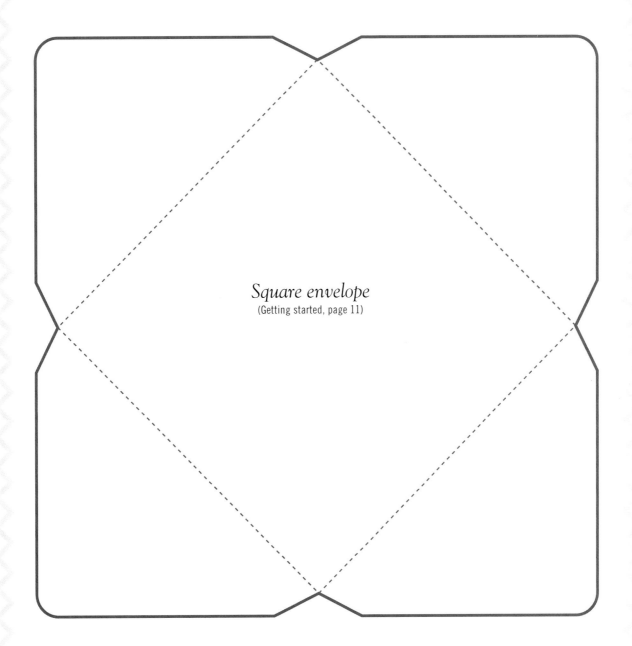

Square envelope
(Getting started, page 11)

SUPPLIERS

US

Michael's Arts & Crafts
8000 Bent Branch Drive
Irving, TX 75063
Tel: (214) 409-1300
Web site:
 http://www.michaels.com
Check the Yellow pages or
their web site for the location
nearest you.

Hobby Lobby
7707 SW 44th Street
Oklahoma City, OK 73179
Tel: (405) 745-1100
Web site:
 http://www.hobbylobby.com
Check the Yellow pages or
their web site for the location
nearest you.

Rugg Road Paper
105 Charles Street
Boston, MA 02114
Tel: (617) 742-0002
(Decorative papers and
stationery supplies)

Kate's Paperie
1282 Third Ave
New York, NY 10021
Tel: (212) 396-3670
Fax: (212) 941-9560
Email:
 info@katespaperie.com
(Decorative papers and
stationery supplies)

Quill-It
P.O. Box 1304-CSS
Elmhurst, IL 60126
Tel: (630) 834-5371
(Quilling papers and kits)

Judi-Kins
17803 South Harvard Blvd
Gardena, CA 90248
Tel: (310) 515-1115
Fax: (310) 323-6619

Web site:
http://www.judikins.com
(Rubber stamps and stamping
supplies)

UNITED KINGDOM

Craft Creations
Ingersoll House
Delamare Road
Cheshunt
Herts EN8 9ND
Tel: (01992) 781 900
Fax: (01992) 634 339
E-mail:
 enquiries@craftcreations.com

The Stencil Store
Head Office
20/21 Heronsgate Road
Chorleywood
Herts WD3 5BN
Tel: (01923) 285577

All Night Media
First Class Stamps Limited
1A George Edwards Road
Fakenham
Norfolk NR21 8NJ
Tel: (01328) 852 600
Fax: (01328) 852 601
E-mail:
 bunnymail@firstclassstamps.
 co.uk
http://www.firstclassstamps.co.uk
(Embossing, stamping and shaker
materials)

The English Stamp Co.
Worth Matravers
Dorset BH19 3JP
For mail order phone
Tel: (01929) 439 117
(Seahorse stamp page 54)

Paperchase
213 Tottenham Court Road
London W1P 9AF
Tel: (020) 7580 8496

or
St Mary's Gate
Manchester
Tel: (0161) 839 1500
(Wide range of papers and
products related to card making)

Specialist Crafts Ltd
Homecrafts Direct
P.O. Box 38
Leicester LE1 9BU
Tel: (0116) 251 3139
Fax: (0116) 251 5015
E-mail:
 post@speccrafts.demon.co.uk
(Quilling tool on page 59; wide
range of crafts supplies)

SOUTH AFRICA

Crafty Supplies
Shop UG 104, The Atrium
Main Road
Claremont, Cape Town
Tel: (021) 671 0286
Fax: (021) 671 0308

Le Papier du Port
Gardens Centre
Gardens, Cape Town
Tel: (021) 462 4796
Mail order:
PO Box 50055
Waterfront 8002

Art, Crafts & Hobbies
72 Hibernia Street
George
Tel/Fax: (044) 874 1337
Mail order:
PO Box 9635
George 6530

Bowker Arts and Crafts
52 Fourth Avenue
Newton Park
Port Elizabeth
Tel: (041) 365 2487
Fax: (041) 365 5306

Art Mates
Shop 313
Musgrave Centre
124 Musgrave Road
Durban
Tel/Fax: (031) 21 0094
Mail ordering service
available

**L & P Stationery and Artists'
Requirements**
65b Church Street
Bloemfontein
Tel: (051) 430 3061
Fax: (051) 448 3242
or
141a Zastron Street
Bloemfontein
Tel: (051) 430 1085
Fax: (051) 430 4102

Art Mates
Shop 313, Musgrave Centre
124 Musgrave Road
Durban
Tel/Fax: (031) 21 0094
Mail ordering service available

Artistea
18b Menlyn Shopping Centre
Atterbury Road
Menlopark, Pretoria
Tel: (012) 348 6121
Fax: (012) 348 6433
Mail order:
PO Box 25902
Monument Park 0105

Southern Arts and Crafts
Flat no. 5
105 Main Street
Rosettenville, Johannesburg
Tel/Fax: (011) 683 6566

The Craftsman
Shop 10, Progress House
110 Bordeaux Drive
Randburg
Tel: (011) 787 1846
Fax: (011) 886 0441

ACKNOWLEDGEMENTS

AUSTRALIA

Lincraft
Gallery Level
Imperial Arcade
Pitt Street
Sydney NSW 2000
Tel: (02) 9221 5111
or
303 Lt Collins Street
Melbourne
VIC 3000
Tel: (03) 9650 1609
or
Queen Street
Brisbane
QLD 4000
Tel: (07) 3221 0064

Alderson Arts and Crafts
64-68 Violet Street
Revesby
NSW 2212
Tel: (02) 9772 1066

Edgeworth Craft Supplies
63 Edgeworth David Avenue
Waitara, NSW
Tel: (02) 9489 3909

Craft Warehouse Shop
Campbell Street
Bowen Hills
QLD 4006
Tel: (07) 3257 1739

NEW ZEALAND

Specialist Suppliers:

Gordon Harris, Art and Graphic Supplies
4 Gillies Ave
Newmarket, Auckland
Tel: (09) 520 4466,
Fax: (09) 520 0880

Studio Art Supplies
81 Parnell Rise
Parnell, Auckland
Tel: (09) 377 0302,
Fax: (09) 377 7657

General Suppliers:

Whitcoulls
Stores throughout
New Zealand

Paper Plus
Stores throughout
New Zealand

This book is the result of my dedicated Funky Eclectica team without whom it would not have materialized! Much time, effort and patience has gone into the card designs shown in this book and I would like to take this opportunity to thank all my friends, family and colleagues for their support and wonderful encouragement.

The Funky team, particularly my assistants Lucy Cooper and Karen Stephens who work with me in the studio every day and helped design and make the cards under our name, whilst under pressure when we were very busy anyway! Our combined humour saw us through! A big thank you today and always.

To all the artists who make up Funky Eclectica past, present and future! We called up some old contacts and friends and put in some brand new artists for an eclectic mix! Namely Tracey Anne Turner, Amanda Caines, Dawn Ireland, Caroline Dent, Nadia Moncrieff, Lucinda Beatty, Rowena Burton, Kathryn Ferrier, Kate Twelvetrees, Alison Orr, Emma Angel, Zoe Ryan, Mandy Jane Middleton, Kate Horeman, Julie Nicols, Ruth and Ria at RaRa, Zara McKenzie and Jan Grayson.

Special thanks to all at NHP who worked with us especially Rosemary for her direction input and fingers, Anke for her card designs and Shona for the photographs. Chiu Mei and Nick Stephens need a mention for their tireless support and enthusiasm and for keeping us on our toes with their amazing organization. Thank you, Chiu, for letting us use one of your designs on the front cover. You are always an inspiration to the Funky team and make things worthwhile!

Special thanks to my Mum for letting me use a glamorous photo of her and to both her and Dad for always being there.

Phil Wood for taking my photograph and more importantly for being the light of my life and believing in me and all my mad endeavours and keeping my spirit free.

Mandy Welch and Wyndham Hollis for their help with embossing, stamping and shaker materials from All Night Media.

Finally to my brother Steve for putting up with me and my moaning and my chaotic business and keeping it all in order!

INDEX